The Courage Within

The Courage Within

Shade Sabitu

WILLOW BOOKS

Unless otherwise indicated, Scripture quotations are taken from the King James Version (KJV) or the New King James Version (NKJV).

Published by Willow Books, Newark, DE 19702.
Direct all inquires to publications@willowbooks.com

Editor: Amelia Cole
Author's Photograph: Titilope Asafa
Front Cover & Packaging: Willow Books
Cover Image: Gombik

Paperback ISBN: 978-0-9990497-4-7

Also available in E-book

Content

Foreword

"Be strong and of good courage." There was something about those words that would leave me feeling weak and intimidated - the exact opposite of what I was supposed to feel. Not to say I never felt the encouragement and empowerment those words were trying to pass along. But for the most part, my thoughts about that instruction were that of inadequacy. These words are supposed to inspire me to stand firm and to face situations and circumstances head on. But what was I doing instead? Doubting my strengths (physical and mental), skills, talents, and whatever else I assumed it meant to 'be strong and of good courage'.

When I'm feeling particularly cheeky, I try to convince myself that these words were technically not directed at me, therefore it wasn't something I needed to worry about. Technically, these words of encouragement, found in Joshua 1:7, were spoken by God to Joshua - a very long time ago, I might add.

Moses, the man who led the Israelites out of Egypt, had died and Joshua was taking over. God spoke those words to him as a way to get him ready for the great task of leading His people. It's almost like being called to be the President of a nation, which in itself, is an extremely challenging role. But Joshua was called to lead a group of individuals that had a history of being unruly, flaky, and insatiable. God knew, more than anything else, Joshua needed to distance himself from the lies called weakness, fear, intimidation, and inadequacy. In essence, all the emotions that would limit him in this extraordinary role. How else would he succeed? How else could he lead such a unique group of people?

So, you see, in my cheeky mind, this instruction was for a different person, from a different era. It was just a story. But I'm sure I can cut through the suspense and speak plainly to you. These words, "be strong and of good courage", were not meant just for Joshua. I deeply believe, more than ever, they were meant for every single one of us. Other than not feeling inadequate or fearful, what does it mean for us to be courageous?

Courage is deciding not to be afraid and acting on that decision. That's it. Pretty easy and straightforward, right? Well, obviously not quite. If courage was that easy, everyone would be living courageously, and we would be living in a completely different kind of world right now - a world where the concept of fear would be as foreign as extraterrestrial life on Mars. But I've found the combination of these two individual parts – 'not being afraid' and 'following through' – extremely challenging for most of us. Sometimes we profess with our lips that we're not afraid of facing our fears, but we then cower at the point where actions meet words. It's one thing to say, for instance, that I'm going to leave an abusive relationship and face the fear of loneliness, and it's another to walk through the door. It suddenly becomes an extraordinary feat when we observe an individual doing the one thing they said they were afraid of doing.

However, to work through either one of these parts, you need a particular superpower. This superpower allows you to 1) reject the lies told to you by fear and 2) have hope of a positive outcome when we perform the required action. I call this a superpower because great things happen when it is utilized, but it can be pretty rare to come across. It isn't rare because only a few people have a monopoly over this superpower. It's rare because only a few people choose to own it. It is a power made available to anyone willing. But sadly, not everyone is willing.

This superpower is called Faith. Some know it as the opposite of fear, but its powers allow for more than the rejection of fear. It allows for the possibility of something better when you pursue your resolve with action. And I'm here to assure you that this faith is available to you. It has always been there. Just think of it as buried treasure. And with this devotional and your Bible, X marks the spot. It is our duty to dig it up and display its beauty. God never intended for us to be afraid or intimidated by anything. He, therefore, planted certain strengths, talents and gifts within us, right from the start, to get us ready to boldly face anything that could ever attempt to scare us. (Jeremiah 1:5) So, it's not right for us to cower with fear. It's against our very nature and the way God made us. It is not in our design to be afraid (2 Timothy 1:7). Anything contrary to that truth is a lie. The truth is we've always had what it takes to face fear and act with courage.

Have you ever been so confused or intimidated by a certain question or problem that you just did nothing? Well that must end today. Not being courageous is actually against God's instruction. We just can't be afraid and decide to do nothing. No longer must we allow an issue or challenge to incapacitate us to the point where we're too afraid to make decisions and act accordingly. I'm not trying to convince you to try; I want you to actually do something. God expects that you do something.

That's the essence of this devotional. An exploration of courage through the eyes of people like Josiah, Abigail, Ruth and a few other characters in the Bible who were faced with challenges, similar to ours, and had to be strong and courageous enough to push back against the lie to turn around, give up, or just do nothing. They didn't have special gifts or talents that made it any easier for them to choose the path of courage. They just decided and acted. And they each did it in their own way. You can and must make courage work for you.

I find originality to be the most exciting thing about courage. The expression of courage has no definition and no boundaries. You get to express courage specifically the way God created you to express it. We have history books, and of course The Bible, to show us examples of how ordinary people defied fear and intimidation and showed courage. Some of us even have family members that we can reference. My parents left all they knew behind to come to a country that presented a better opportunity for themselves and their children. They had no relatives or friends nearby but decided to do it because it was the courageous thing for them to do. A teenage girl encouraging her friends to sit with the new girl during lunch is showing courage. She could be mocked or ostracized by those same friends, but she cheats fear because she wants a new person to feel welcomed. It's those simple acts that show our courage.

The stories in this devotional should therefore only serve as sources of inspiration. I don't expect you to express courage the same way these individuals did. In fact, if you do, you would be doing a major disservice to yourself, to the gifts and talents God put in you, and to the whole world. Yes, the world! You may not know this yet, but we all need you to express your courage in the way God has created you to express it, not only for your sake but for ours too. (Romans 8:19) So, be ready to be different. Be ready to stand out. But more importantly, be ready to experience change in yourself and the world around you. Not in the 'Superman saved the world from an asteroid' kind of way. But in a "hey, stop bullying that little girl" kind of way. A "let me pray with you right here, right now" kind of way. Remember, it's the little steps, the here and now, that makes the world shift a little closer to where we need it to be. It's us living courageously out loud that will reduce fear and intimidation to mere words on a page. So, if you've decided to pick up this book, let it inspire you to take the next step and ask God for your own expression of courage.

I will warn you though. Being courageous is not a one-and-done activity. Courage is a journey. And like most journeys, there will be high points and low ones. You'll be faced with moments that will require you to step in (face fear), step out (shun intimidation), step up (act fearlessly), or step down (humbly ask for help). Your decision to be courageous will be tested constantly. Your stance will always be questioned. Your position on certain matters will make you and others uncomfortable. But it must not stop you from making those daily decisions to move ahead.

Courage is also a call to serve others, which you'll notice in the pages to come. It's a call to do more than just pursue good for oneself. Think about it for a second. Speaking out against abuse committed towards you will not only shed light on those shadows in your own life, but it will enable the strength in others to identify and act against such abuse in their own lives. Courage begets courage. So, if you've ever thought, "how can I be a blessing to others?", one way is to answer courageously to your calling.

But be encouraged; there will always be a reward. No one who has ever crossed over into the courage lane has regretted the decision. You'll start to notice that things will begin to fall in place once you step into courage. You'll even notice an increase in your compassion and love for others; an increased peace knowing you're living out your calling; an increased strength to tackle new challenges; increased joy and hope knowing things are getting better; and much more. It is impossible to bless others without being blessed yourself.

Will it get hard? Yes. Will you have setbacks? Most likely. Will you completely rid yourself of every lie called fear and intimidation? Not a chance. I mean, if all those things went away, how else would you grow? How else would you get to experience the hidden treasures inside you?

What I'm about to say should make you feel much better though. Joshua 1:9 says, *"Have I not commanded you? Be strong and of good courage; do not be afraid, nor be dismayed, for the Lord your God is with you wherever you go?"* You will not be on this journey alone. You'll have God with you; sending help your way, picking you up when you fall, and giving you joy in your accomplishments. It's not going to be an easy ride, but it won't be a lonely one. As Henry Ford once said, "Those who walk with God always reach their destination."

So, I implore you, please take this journey. It's never too early or too late to be courageous. Invest your heart and your time. Determine within your heart that this journey will be worth it. It may help to literally write those words down. THIS JOURNEY WILL BE WORTH IT. Because it will be. It's a promise. I'm on this journey as well. I'll be praying for you and cheering you on. I'll also be listening out for your cheers for me. So, strap in and let's get ready to show some courage. With God on our side, we got this!

With much love,

Shade

Using This Devotional

Do not feel the pressure to rush through the chapters of this book. In my life, I've noticed that learning too many lessons at once diminishes each lesson's impact. Why? Information overload. For a lesson to stick, I need it to materialize itself in a special way, so I can fully grasp its meaning. When I was younger, my dad would say things like, "I'll explain it to you when you get older." I remember how frustrated I felt because I believed I could handle whatever he was withholding from me at the time. But now, I see how some lessons are better learned with maturity and the right headspace to fully and properly digest it. So, take your time. Read each chapter and think about how each story impacts you in the moment. You may even need to revisit certain chapters at a later date.

You may wonder, "But what if the lesson in a particular chapter is not quite for me?" Well, you may be right. Some of these acts of courage may not fit with who you are. Maybe you don't have friends that are undeserving of grace, or maybe you've already won the battle of unforgiveness in your life. Well then, feel free to share those learnings with someone else.

You'll notice that each chapter follows the same outline. Here's what each section addresses:

Picture this!

The goal of this section is to paint a modern-day problem and see how we can use the lessons learned from our Biblical brothers and sisters to help address the issue. Modern meets ancient here. Some of the situations in this section are real life stories, some are fictional, and some are even poems tackling the subject of the chapter. Names, characters, businesses, places, events, and incidents are either abridged versions of headline news stories, or fictitious products of my imagination. For the fictitious stories, any resemblance to actual persons, living or dead, or actual events is purely coincidental, not preconceived and certainly not intended.

The story

I take the main characters of the chapter and describe their stories in a simple and understandable way. Most of these stories will lack the details I felt were not pertinent to the point being addressed in the chapter, but I welcome readers to read the character's full story by checking the reference under *Check it out.*

Courage on display

In this section, we get into why the character's actions were courageous. Understanding the significance of these actions, as it relates to courage, will help you to also evaluate your own actions and how your actions may be thought of as courageous.

CHARACTER PROFILE

What were these Bible characters like? What character traits did they have that made them behave the way they did? This section will help you realize how similar you may be to these individuals and hopefully encourage you to act as courageously as they did. Are you naturally curious? Maybe Josiah's story will inspire you to search out some truths of your own. Or maybe you're the stubborn and enterprising type. The way Ruth stood by her mother-in-law, Naomi, might make you think, "oh yeah, that's me alright." The traits that characterize us are perfect ingredients that get uniquely mixed together to make an irreplicable dish of wonder. Though your traits may be similar to another's, the outcome of your courage will be unlike what we've seen before.

CHECK IT OUT!

There's something about reading directly from the source that makes the story more impactful. Take the extra step and read the words that inspired the story in the chapter.

THE REWARD

We're all aware that courage comes with risk. But it also comes with a reward. This section helps us identify the reward received by the characters in the Bible story.

PONDER A BIT

The questions in this section will cause you to pause and think. To think about and better understand the characters or act of courage discussed in the chapter. But it will also help you better understand yourself in relation to the topic of the chapter.

ACT NOW

There's nothing like putting newly acquired knowledge to the test. In this section, you'll find some suggestions on how to practice and work through the concept(s) learned in the chapter. I encourage you to come up with ideas of your own, so don't feel restricted to the ones suggested. My suggestions are just a place to start.

EVEN MORE

Did you discover something special when you read the Bible passage yourself? Did the sweet whisper of the Holy Spirit minister another gem to you? Please feel free to share with me by email, shadesabitu@gmail.com

So, get a highlighter, notebook and pen. Use this book as a navigation tool for your own journey to living a more courageous life, or as a study guide with your small group, friends, colleagues, work team, etc. The characters are not profiled in any order of importance. Each person was unique in the way(s) in which they displayed their courage. Study each character and let their stories inspire you to be courageous - in your own way. Jot down your process for navigating these challenges and feel free to share your thoughts with me. I'm sure you will inspire me with your findings. I really look forward to hearing from you.

Chapter 1

Joseph

Courage is forgiving those that hurt us

PICTURE THIS!

Chris had just been offered her first job out of college! She never thought it would happen so quickly. Barely two months post-graduation and there she was with an offer letter to be the newest Data Analyst at Khemie Technology. She was the first person in her group of friends to land a job, a nice paying one at that. She decided to take her friends out for dinner to celebrate and talk about her plans for the new journey.

She worked her way around the table at dinner and answered as many questions as she could about finding the opportunity, scaling through the interview, and her moving plans. The only person that showed little to no interest was Carlos. He'd been shifty all evening, looking at his watch every so often, and feeling more and more uncomfortable with the sound of Chris's voice. Chris remembered Carlos once told her about a cousin of his that lived in Spring Meadow, the town she was moving to. She wanted to know if he could connect them, so his cousin could give her some advice on getting an apartment in the new city. He responded with a weary smile and a one-word answer, "Sure." He avoided her for the rest of the night but was unable to leave the restaurant without Chris demanding a goodbye hug.

She knew he wasn't his regular self throughout the evening, so she decided to ask why he was so distracted. He answered quite sharply, "To be honest, I'm just wondering how someone like you could have landed a job faster than me. My grades were much better, and I interviewed for that same position and wasn't even given a callback!" With that, he turned around and walked briskly away while Chris stood speechless and confused.

Though she had no words to say, her mind was racing a million miles an hour. "Was Carlos mad at me for getting the job he wanted? Did he feel I betrayed him? How was I supposed to know he applied for that job? Why did they choose me over him? Or was he just jealous?" After a while of staring into his direction, she walked towards her car and headed home. On her way home, she found herself saying a word of prayer for Carlos. She prayed he would find something soon enough and not worry about what he thought he lost to her.

Carlos was envious. He couldn't get over his selfish thoughts enough to rejoice and be happy for his friend. Envy and jealousy, as emotions, are not foreign with humans. Children as young as two have been observed to show signs of envy when a sibling or friend has something desirable but seemingly unattainable. But as people age, and wisdom grows, people tend to understand that envy and jealousy are unhealthy and that these emotions can lead to hatred and evil intentions.

In the Bible, there's an account of a young man who experienced the brutal dangers of envy and jealousy. This person was Joseph. His brothers treated him badly because of their envy of him, subjecting him to a very hard life. But, as we'll read in the next few paragraphs, his response to their envy was the exact opposite of what they probably deserved.

<hr>

THE STORY

For those of you who have spent any amount of time in children's Sunday school, the story of Joseph's life may sound pretty familiar. He was the boy who was dearly loved by his father and given a coat of many colors as a token of that love. He wasn't an only child though; he had ten older (step)brothers, one younger brother, and several (step)sisters. Back in those days, a man was recognized by the number of sons he had, so the number of Jacob's daughters was never emphasized in the Bible. And it wasn't one of those, "but I love you all equally" kind of deals. Joseph's father, Jacob, really did love Joseph a lot more than his siblings, making his brothers extremely jealous of him. And as it sometimes happens, their jealousy led to their complete hatred of him.

Not only was he favored by their father, Joseph would sometimes rat out his brothers, and torment them with his dreams of one day ruling over them. So, in a way, you can say their envy and hatred was justified. In reality, nothing justifies hate or envy, but using a more appropriate word like 'rationalized' may not capture how most of us argue our reasons for holding onto past hurts committed against us. But we'll get back to this in a moment.

Fast forward to a day when motive finally met opportunity. The brothers were in a perfect position to kill Joseph and be done with him and his dreams once and for all. But they eventually decided to sell him off as a slave instead. This way, they could get rid of him without having blood on their hands. Plus, they would make some money by getting rid of their source of anger; that's what most of us would call a win-win.

So, in a single moment, Joseph went from the favored son to being a slave, all because his brothers decided to act on their envy of him. See, that's the problem with jealousy; it breeds hatred, which then leads to the destruction of life. In the short term, it may look like the only affected and destroyed party is the subject of the envy; but eventually, the destroyed life is that of the envious person. I digress again though; back to the story.

From the time Joseph left the presence of his brother, he lived in Egypt as a slave and was then jailed for something he didn't do. But the whole time, God's presence was with him. The Bible notes that he even prospered in these various situations. Isn't it strange to think of a person succeeding as a slave or a person in captivity? But because God favored Joseph, he was able to have peace and prospered in his trials.

Then the time of promise finally came. Pharaoh had a problem only Joseph could solve. And because of this, Pharaoh made Joseph his next-in-command. So, again, in a single moment, Joseph went from slave and felon to VP of Egypt. It's truly amazing how a single event or decision can change the trajectory of our lives.

A great famine came upon the Earth and food was hard to come by. However, because of Joseph's great wisdom and leadership, Egypt had enough food stored up. Egypt even had enough to sell to others from foreign lands. But all those who wanted to buy food had to go through Joseph. Then one day, a group of ten men showed up before Joseph. In humility and reference, they bowed before Joseph and pleaded with him to sell them grain. They were Joseph's brothers! He recognized them but they didn't recognize him.

So, here he was, in a position to pay them back for the hardship of 13 years. He had the power and motive to deny their request, send them to jail, or even kill them. But he chose a path his brothers didn't choose when they too had power and motive. He chose love. He chose compassion. He chose to bless them and give them life. He chose forgiveness.

COURAGE ON DISPLAY

Forgiving someone is easier said than done. It may even be the hardest, non-physical thing most of us will have to do in our lives. I'm sure every single person reading this chapter can think of at least one time in their lives when they were deeply hurt or treated unfairly by someone else. The pain of those actions usually isn't as bad if we feel we deserved what they did. But man does it feel horrible when you did nothing to deserve the ill-treatment.

Depending on who you ask, Joseph may or may not have deserved the ill-treatment he faced at the hands of his brothers. But we can all agree they acted out of envy and hatred, and actions that stem from those feelings are never justified. Unfortunately, neither hatred nor jealousy can ever be cured by seeing the destruction of your target.

The satisfaction obtained from seeing the other person miserable is neither full nor permanent.

And just as jealousy is not cured by hurting the object of your envy, offenses can never be cured by unforgiveness. The emotional abuse of holding on to hurt goes from being an affliction put upon us, to one we impose on ourselves. It becomes an abuse that keeps tormenting our souls until we decide to let go. Unlike what they say about time, we can't rely on it to heal all our wounds.

If we imagine the hurt as a severe open leg wound, we may better understand the power of actively addressing our hurt and forgiving our trespassers, versus ignoring the issue and passively letting time do some mediocre version of healing for us. A person who deals with the hurt directly can be likened to someone who medicates the wound. The wound heals and closes up more quickly than if it were left to the mercy of time.

Both ways of addressing the problem are painful, and side effects exist in each scenario, but the overall outcomes differ in the long-term. Bruised egos, raw emotions, denial of the wrong committed, excuses, finger pointing, non-redeemable time spent over unproductive discussions, perceived or actual manipulation, and unrepentant behavior, are just some of those side effects of a direct effort to deal with the hurt. These are painful to deal with, of course, but are mostly temporary emotions or behaviors. The courageous person will discover the pain of directness is faster, more efficient, and will reduce the scar tissue left behind. However, the side effects of passively letting time pass by the hurt can be more severe and prolonged. Misunderstandings, assumed enemies, numbness to love, loss of joy, depression, and hatred are those longer-term effects of a passive engagement with our hurt.

You may notice scars left behind in both scenarios. But depending on how the wound was addressed, the scars will tell different stories. The scar from the medicated wound means victory. It brings gratitude, an appreciation for growth, and an increased capacity to love and deal with new challenges. The scar from an unattended wound is usually uglier in appearance, manifesting in unresolved anger, hurtful outbursts, bitterness towards people who are like the offender, the feeling of betrayal, distrust of people, cynicism, and/or hopelessness.

Forgiveness is a challenge, and that is why it is truly an act of courage. It starts from a position of, "I'm completely comfortable in this space of being mad at you, ignoring you, talking bad about you, and retaliating against you, all the while looking wise to all those that know of the hurt you've caused me", but then elevating to the place where the thought process is "You've bruised my heart/body/ego, and though it is extremely painful to step out of this box of hate, to venture into a space where I will look foolish for loving you or being kind to you, I will anyway because I know it blesses you, me, and others."

So why did Joseph forgive his brothers? Because he was a courageous leader. I'm sure he must have asked himself two important questions. 1) "What do I stand to gain by retaliating against my brothers?" And 2) "What do I stand to gain by forgiving them? To which he would answer, "nothing and everything," respectively. He weighed the outcome of his potential actions and decided to take the path of life.

The one thing you may not have thought about is that his forgiveness was a life-altering, precious gift to his brothers. Their actions were driven by hate and envy. His was driven by compassion and love. Here he was in a position to retaliate, but instead he decided to give life and elevate the ones that hurt him. He didn't let his ego get in the way of doing for them what may have seemed foolish to others.

Joseph also realized his brothers were, ultimately, not his enemies; hate and envy were. And there was no way for him to defeat those enemies with anything else but love and forgiveness. Despite all the obstacles, and all the attempts to thwart his dreams, Joseph finally saw his dreams manifest before his very eyes. So, in the end, hate and envy had no effect on him. They were just boulders that his brothers rolled into his path. But these boulders were unable to block him from getting to his destination.

There are those in our own lives that may remain unrepentant or will never acknowledge the wrong they've done. In as much as forgiveness is easier when there's a sincere apology as a prefix, our forgiveness should never be dependent on someone else's request to be forgiven. In Joseph's story, he never gave his brothers the opportunity to ask for his forgiveness before he gave it. He gave it to them out of his own desire to love them. His forgiveness did not depend on them; it was his gift to give. They did not deserve or earn it, and a majority of people who hurt us will not deserve or earn our forgiveness either. But the choice to forgive is a decision we make in spite of the other person.

For Joseph, the alternative would be to see them suffer and languish in pain which, he concluded, wouldn't have served any one any good. So like Joseph, we should always ask ourselves, "what do I stand to gain by hurting them back?" What do I stand to gain by blessing them instead?"

Character profile

- Patient
- Faithful
- Disciplined
- Possessed foresight
- Visionary
- Consistent

Check it out!

Genesis 37-45

The Reward

- Joseph's gift of forgiveness resulted in the rescue of a whole nation from starvation during the time of widespread famine.
- Jacob, who was grieved because he thought for many years that he had lost his beloved son, was reunited with Joseph and able to live his last years with all his sons.

Ponder a bit

- Have you ever felt envious of someone else's accomplishments? If so, how did you respond to those feelings? If not, what feelings do you have when you see someone doing or having something you truly desire but you are unable to acquire at that moment?
- What is the one thing someone could do to you that would seem completely unforgivable?
- What are some things that you've done to someone that weren't a big deal to you but hurt them deeply? Did you ask for forgiveness? Were you forgiven?

Act Now

1. There are some exercises that are recommended for those of us with stage fright. The point of most of these exercises is to take back the power unintentionally given to the audience and channel it in a way that gives you strength to address the crowd. I encourage you to take the spirit behind this concept and apply it the next time you see your 'enemy', or the person you can't forgive. Take back your power and channel it in a way that strengthens you to separate the sin from the person. Approach them and tell them you've forgiven them for their offense towards you. It doesn't matter if they agree with you or not. The exercise gives you strength and

peace, and if that's the only outcome, it's enough.

2. If you know you've hurt someone, ask for their forgiveness. Make it easier for them to bless you and themselves with the gift of forgiveness.

3. Develop the habit of being happy for others. Congratulate people when they achieve something great. Thank God for those that get the one thing you've been praying for. Pray to God that He'll bless you in your own time. God's blessings are abundant and limitless. If He did it for them, He can do it for you.

EVEN MORE

Chapter 2

Peter

Courage is stepping out in the face of fear

PICTURE THIS!

It wasn't too late for Kendall and Lola to drop their pens and walk out of the counselor's office. There was no shame in saying they weren't ready for the challenges ahead of them. Their friends had shared the blessings of adoption but were also not shy about sharing the challenges they faced going through the adoption process. They both looked at themselves and tried to read each other's thoughts. Was this the path they really wanted to travel down?

Everything else in their lives was lining up exactly where Kendall and Lola wanted it to be. Kendall was a Public Relations consultant and his business had a growing list of clients. He even had two talented guys on staff that could keep things moving if he needed to step away for a week or two to care for a new baby. Lola was a registered nurse and knew she could work out a flexible schedule if the need arose as well. They had eager family members that lived close by and would be willing to pitch in. All they needed now was the baby.

Trying to get pregnant on their own already proved to be draining - physically, emotionally, and financially. They tried not to think of the numerous IVF treatments they had endured. They finally gave in to the idea of adoption but were beginning to doubt whether they had the capacity to deal with the unique challenges that came with it. They truly longed for children, but the road to having them seemed to get more and more complicated and unwieldy. There were no guarantees that they would end up with a baby, even if they did take the leap of faith and begin the adoption process. It could end up being a huge investment with absolutely no return.

In the Bible, there was a guy named Peter who found himself desiring something incredible, but knowing in order to get to that object, he would need to face some tumultuous obstacles. But he also knew he needed to step out of his comfort zone and into the unknown for him to get to his destination. His story should inspire us all to step out into, and even embrace, the unknown obstacles, the uncharted path, and the imperfect circumstances that will line the path to our desired destination. If Peter can do it, then we should all be encouraged to face the unknown and be willing to get out of our 'boats'.

THE STORY

There was a recent story in the headlines about a cruise ship that was caught in a particularly bad storm. In the associated video, you can see dinner tables and chairs moving in the direction of the wavering tilts. Guests were understandably terrified and unsure of what would happen next. There was nowhere to go, and they were at the mercies of the wind. Luckily for them, the weather became more favorable and they were able to reach land in one piece. One piece physically; I'm sure their mental state was, at the very least, slightly altered.

Now picture a vessel not as big or as sophisticated as a cruise ship, but still caught in a similar kind of storm. Then add the unexpected element of seeing your friend walking towards the boat you're in - on top of these raging seas! The one word that describes this scenario is impossible.

Well, this is the scene created for us with the story of Jesus walking on water. The story started at the end of another incredible event - about 5,000 men (and probably a similar number of women and children) fed with five loaves of bread and two fish. I won't dwell on the details of that particular story, but you can imagine it was a challenge trying to get rid of such a large group of people after being fed in such a miraculous way.

Anyway, Jesus needed to disperse the group but also wanted his disciples to get a head start on their next destination. So, he sent the disciples ahead in a boat while he took care of the crowd. Once the people were gone, he was finally able to step away and pray with some peace and quiet. When he was done praying, he started to head in the direction of his disciples, who were already at sea. In the meantime, the disciples found themselves mid-sea in the middle of a turbulent storm.

All of a sudden, the disciples see someone walking towards the boat - on top of the water. And while I have absolutely no idea what exactly was going through their minds, we can all safely assume they were freaked out. Seeing their panicked faces, the Water-Walker knew he had to call out to assure them he was not a ghost, but their leader and friend, Jesus. "Hey guys, don't be afraid. It's just me, Jesus!" He said. But I can imagine that their response was most certainly not "Oh yeah! It's just Jesus. Nothing to worry about here." Something tells me their minds were not put at ease by his utterance.

Almost as a way to convince himself of what he was seeing and hearing, Peter cried out to Jesus, saying, "Lord, if it's you, command me to come to you on the water." To that, Jesus responded, "Come." And with that simple instruction, Peter stepped out of the boat and starts to walk on the water towards Jesus.

Courage on display

Most of us have a great ability to visualize greatness. We can see ourselves in situations better than what we're experiencing in the moment. And we usually follow those visions with deep feelings of hope for the manifestation of these visions and dreams. We see ourselves in loving relationships, living in excellent health, having access to limitless resources, traveling the globe, having our own children, giving to the needy, finding a cure to an incurable disease, having fulfilling careers, or not having to work at all. These desires are always associated with an expectation of endless joy.

But unfortunately and fortunately, there's a gap between where we are and where our visions take us. This space is what most of us are unable to see clearly; this space is the place where we usually struggle. We don't know how big or long this space is, and we can't predict the distance with absolute certainty. It appears dark and unsteady, like the waters Peter stepped onto. But like Peter, we must step out of our current state and onto the uncharted pathway, in defiance of its ruggedness, if we're going to get to where we want to be.

In Peter's case, it definitely helped that Jesus called out to Peter and invited him to come into that darkness. Such voices are what we need sometimes to take that leap of faith. A voice that encourages us to take the step, to not lose faith, to lift us up when we begin to entertain self-doubt and sink into despair. But we need to realize that most times that voice will be calling to us from the inside. This voice is the Holy Spirit. You may be expecting your external cheering quad (family, friends, coworkers, church members, others in your boat) to encourage you to step out in faith and tackle those challenges standing between you and your dreams, but if these folks can't or don't show up, it shouldn't stop us from moving.

I would be remiss if I didn't tell you that Peter, at some point in his story, stopped walking on the water and started to fall through. But Jesus immediately grabbed his hand, saved him and proceeded to tell Peter what he suddenly did wrong (all signs of a great leader, by the way). Jesus revealed to Peter that there was a sudden but significant change in his state of mind; a change from courage and great faith to that of fear and disbelief. Once Peter started to doubt what he was doing, he started to slip. If Peter kept up with his initial courageous thinking, he would have covered a great distance on the water with Jesus.

Sometimes, like Peter, we may start a new adventure with so much courage, faith, and steam. But once our confidence shifts, and we let doubt creep its way into our thinking, we suddenly start to sink. Inwardly, we entertain feelings of anxiety, anger, frustration, and self-doubt; outwardly, our attitude can range from the extremes of anger to that of overconfidence. Usually, what we need to do is retrace our steps back to that initial place of courage and fearlessness. It is at this place of faith that we can regain our footing again.

Jesus was the place of peace for Peter. His eyes were fixed on him when he took his first step. But once his eyes wandered over to the turmoil going on around him, he suddenly was going in the opposite direction of where he wanted to be. Instead of moving forward, he was sinking downwards. Once you find yourself heading in the wrong direction, you need to shift your eyes back on your goal; back on Jesus. That is when and where you will find the hand you need to lift you back up and get you moving forward again.

Like Peter, embrace the uncertainty that you know is around you. Embrace the chaos that will line the road to your dreams. But block your ears to the noise of the thunder and listen to the still small voice telling you to "Come". Let the mighty winds be the boost that will move you forward to your dream. Keep your eyes on your destination and let courage keep you moving in the right direction.

CHARACTER PROFILE
- Curious
- Confident
- Fearless

CHECK IT OUT!
Matthew 14:22-33

THE REWARD
- Peter did the remarkable. There were others in the boat who were too afraid to step out onto the waters. But Peter's single act of courage allowed him to experience something his peers never did.
- Peter's act of faith was an avenue for God to show the disciples that they were truly being led by the Son of God. It validated their faith and renewed their trust in God.

PONDER A BIT
- Can you remember a time when you stepped out in faith and did something remarkable? What was going on in your mind at the time?

- What are some situations you've avoided because the thought of the obstacles you could face prevented you from even trying?
- What are some common situations that typically seem bleak from the onset but eventually turn out great?

ACT NOW

1. Think about the desires you have for yourself. Create a dream board. Write out some of your thoughts in a journal. Then take one of those things and find out what the first step of that journey will be. Don't dwell too much on the next step until you've completed step 1. Then take each step and tackle them one after the other. Write out the journey- the things you're learning along the way - but keep moving until you achieve that goal.

EVEN MORE

Chapter 3

Abigail

Courage is standing up for a friend even when they don't deserve it

PICTURE THIS!

Let's say you have a friend who is not well liked by most people. To be honest, most people see him/her as rude, obnoxious, stuck up, or all of the above. You've known them for years though, and you're able to see past the tough outer layer most people aren't patient enough to tolerate. Yes, you've also had those moments when you've doubted your reasons for loving them. But through it all, you've stayed by their side like the great friend you are. The whole world thinks you're a saint for calling such a person a friend. They wonder why such a good-natured individual like you would even bother yourself with such a crude person.

Well, now imagine this friend is your spouse. This crude, unfriendly individual is the person you live with and see every day. Of course, you're used to their ways, and even know what to expect and how to deal with them. But their behavior still rubs others the wrong way, even to the point where these people may want to hurt your spouse. This was Abigail's situation, and she needed courage to stand up for her spouse when he decided to take his unpleasantness a bit too far, getting himself in big trouble. Though, he brought the problem upon himself, Abigail was the one to help him get out of it. Here's Abigail's story.

THE STORY

Abigail was married to an unpleasant man named Nabal. In one version of the Bible, the word used to describe him was "scoundrel". Not only was Nabal mean-spirited, he was also very wealthy, and his temperament hindered him from being a blessing to others. He was selfish and even ungrateful when others did favors for him. Abigail, on the other hand, was known as being both beautiful and wise (beauty and brains). Even those who worked for her husband knew she was the one to approach for wise counsel. She was easy to talk to and very charismatic.

The time of harvest had come and Nabal was gearing up for some major feasting. David, the young man appointed to be the next King of Israel, had recently protected Nabal's shepherds while they tended to their animals in the wilderness. Now, tending to sheep is no small feat. And tending to sheep in the wilderness was a great challenge for the shepherds. They were only able to do their job because David and his men protected and shielded them from the dangers of such an environment. David learned of Nabal's great harvest and feasting plans and sent word to Nabal to spare some food for him and his men that were still in the wilderness. It was a minor request given what David and his men did for Nabal's shepherds. Unfortunately, Nabal not only ignored the request but insulted David and his men in the process. He lacked the concern, kindness, and respect David had shown him in the months before.

David's response was laden with fury. He couldn't understand how Nabal could be so callous, disrespectful and ungrateful. His decision was to destroy Nabal and anything of value to him. He got his men ready for war and headed for Nabal's house. Fortunately for Nabal, Abigail got wind of her husband's grave disregard for the soon to be king. Abigail was told of the situation and took actions into her own hands. She prepared gifts for David and his men and ran out to meet them. Upon seeing the charging army, she pleaded for her husband, acknowledged his faults, and persuaded David to rise above the anger he felt towards Nabal. David could see that her words were filled with wisdom and decided against the punishment he had for Nabal. Abigail offered the gifts she prepared for David and his men and sent them on their way.

COURAGE ON DISPLAY

For Abigail, courage meant sticking up for Nabal. Again, the trouble was nothing she caused or brought upon herself. She knew her husband's personality and didn't doubt that he could have offended David with his harsh words. Nabal was at fault, and the consequences of his actions were deserved. However, she was loyal to her spouse, even with his character flaws. Instead of hearing of the impending danger and saving herself or abandoning her husband, she thought of a way to bring peace to the situation. She put herself on the line, pleaded with David, and sought forgiveness on her husband's behalf. (Sounds a lot like what Jesus did for us, doesn't it?) She had enough courage to build a bridge between the two parties at odds with each other when it was probably easier to let Nabal's due punishment come to him.

After all, the text didn't particularly mention that David would harm her. David's focus was on Nabal and other males in the household. Same thing for that unfriendly friend. Insults and anger targeted towards them are usually meant solely for their personal consumption and should not be of any concern to anyone else. However, like Abigail, we should always be concerned about the actions of those around us. Directly or indirectly, she would be impacted by the consequences of Nabal's crudeness. Because of this, we are called to walk the path of courage and confront the problem head-on. It's never going to be easy to stand up for others, especially when they're in the wrong. It's even harder to do when the individual seems to be undeserving of your grace. But Abigail showed us it can be done.

In this story, courage also meant not being weighed down by the cause of the problem but focusing on possible solutions. Abigail knew there was no time for pointing fingers or ascribing blame. She decided what the best course of action was and took action immediately. She approached David, bearing gifts for him and his men, and proceeded to talk him down from his anger. Because of that single act of courage, she saved her husband. She used her gifts of wisdom, boldness, and charisma to change the heart of a person who was determined to destroy him. She literally faced a hard problem head on and ended up putting out a potential wildfire. We should be inspired that a single act of courage can overcome the flaws/faults of our friends and redeem a problematic situation.

Character profile

- Wise
- Charismatic
- Quick decision maker
- Bold
- Influential
- Humble

Check it out!

1 Samuel 25: 2-35

The Reward

- Abigail saved her husband and household.
- Abigail helped David understand the power of overlooking a fault and prevented him from unnecessary bloodshed.
- Abigail later married David and became Queen. (Yeah, weird outcome, but the short version of what happened is that Nabal later died, Abigail became a widow, and David married her.)

Ponder a bit

- Are there people in your life you've been good to but have wronged you in return?

Did you seek revenge or even secretly wish that God would punish them for you?

- What are some ways you can stand up for these individuals? In a group of friends, are we the first ones to share their shortcomings with the group?
- What other lessons did you learn from Abigail story?

ACT NOW

1. Write down the names of those that have wronged you in some way. Speak each name in prayer, asking God to help you release them from your hear.
2. Think of ways you can stand up for these or other people when unkind words are being said about them. It's definitely unpopular to be the one person saying something nice about an unfriendly individual, but it is also very courageous.

EVEN MORE

Chapter 4

Hannah

Courage is honoring vows and keeping promises

Picture this!

Did you know that only 8% of people keep their New Year's resolutions? According to research conducted by the University of Scranton, only a small fraction of people are able to keep the promise of 'a newer and better me' to themselves. In a way, one could easily reason that the soft whispers we speak to ourselves may get ignored after a while because these are usually not associated with reliable accountability checkpoints. There's typically no outward-facing shame that needs to be endured when we break promises to ourselves. Plus, we tend to be quick to justify our lack of commitment to those things we've promised ourselves. I mean, how long can you really stay mad or disappointed with your own self over a teeny-tiny failed promise?

Unfortunately, promises that we make to others don't seem to fare that well either. We start out with good intentions, to do what we say we're going to do. But somewhere along the way, we disconnect ourselves from those promises or from the people we made the promises to. So, I wonder, why do we find it so hard to do the things we said we would do? One thought is that we tend to promise 'too much' - the overpromising, under-delivering problem. We also tend to lose the feelings that we had at the time of the promise; therefore, dissociating our need to keep the promise. And I'm sure there are many more reasons for not following through on our obligations.

The following poems by C.J. Krieger (2019) and Morgan Gregg (2013), respectively, talk about promises:

Promises and Dreams

It was a violent fall storm
Stripping bare all the trees
Except for a few brave leaves
That desperately chose to cling to life
What was a forest filled with green
Had now become a sea of yesterdays summer
And like that leaf that wouldn't let go
He walked in solitude
Through all the promises
That had since
Fallen away

Keeping the Promises

Do you remember, when we were young, those promises we made?
The promise to be there for each other, no matter night or day.

The promise to keep secrets, no matter what they are.
The promise to be friends forever, no matter where we are.

The promise to stand up for each other, no matter what the cause.
The promise to never judge each other, no matter all the flaws.

The promise to always tell the other, they're doing something wrong.
The promise to remember this when the other has sadly gone.

The promise to always help each other, no matter what the weather.
The promise to always keep a promise, from then until forever.

We're older now, we've changed, we've grown, we've forgotten many things. We've lived through life, are facing our end, whatever it may bring.

We've had our problems, doubts, and sorrows, that came along the way.

Yet still we've managed to keep them all, the promises we made.

We should always think of our promises as covenants or contracts that shouldn't be broken, regardless of who we're making the promises to or how we feel at the time of payment. It's better to not promise at all than to promise and fail at the point of redemption. Hannah's story was that of a huge promise made to God. Her pledge was probably one that would seem impossible for most of us to redeem. But she did it anyway. Let's explore Hannah's story, her promise, and the consequence of her keeping her promise.

THE STORY

Hannah longed to have a child of her own. Though her husband, Elkanah, loved her dearly, and did what he could to make her feel cared for, his affection failed to fill the void left by not birthing her own children. Back in those days, it was normal to have more than one wife. Unfortunately for Hannah, Elkanah's other wife, Peninnah, was cruel towards Hannah and taunted her endlessly about her inability to conceive and bear children. As one could guess, Peninnah had many children of her own and thought she had the right to taunt her sister-wife.

And like most situations in which a person is taunted or bullied, Hannah's infertility was something she couldn't control or do anything about. She did the one thing she could do though, and that was pray.

She visited the temple often and prayed year after year. Over the years, it seemed like God wasn't hearing and/or answering her prayers. Until one year, when she decided to take her prayers to another level. If only God could give her one male child, she prayed, even just one, she promised she would turn him back over to God and have him serve before God in his temple all the days of his life.

And wouldn't you know it, God heard and answered her prayer. She had a son and named him Samuel, meaning "I asked God for him." She nursed her baby and waited till he was weaned before she went back to the temple. This was now the moment of truth. Would she leave him at the temple or take him back with her? She finally had a child of her own in a household where she was constantly being tormented by Peninnah. Would she dare return home without the one reason her tormenting stopped? Will Peninnah find something else to taunt her about? Would she have joy again now that she would have to leave her source of joy behind at the temple? Did God really need this child? What was He going to do with a young child anyway?

We can assume any or all of these thoughts crossed her mind. But she pushed past these thoughts and left Samuel at the temple in the care of Eli, the Chief Priest. She was courageous enough to keep her promise to God. In the face of fear, shame, sadness, loneliness, and torment, she kept her promise. Though she didn't know what the future held for her, she kept her promise. But God, being the faithful rewarder of a whole-hearted sacrifice, went on to give her more...more children. God blessed her with five more children! And Samuel went on to become one of the greatest prophets to judge over God's people, the children of Israel.

Courage on display

You read that right. The one child Hannah prayed earnestly for was the same child she promised to give back to God. All she wanted was to experience the joy of motherhood, even if it was just for a short period in her lifetime. She had no other desire or expectation; she only wanted to put her tormentors to shame by accomplishing what they thought was impossible for her. But here she was, being tested beyond what she had bargained for.

How familiar does this sound? When most of us find ourselves praying for the same thing over and over again, or even praying for something really important to us at the moment, we start making desperate promises to God. "If you just land me that dream job, or get me out of this trouble, or get me safely off of this turbulent plane, I'll go to church every Sunday for the rest of my life." But how many times do we actually make good on these promises?

How many times have we made vows to our fellow humans and walked back on those promises? There was a time when people would shake hands on an agreement, and the parties trusted one another to meet the terms of that agreement. Now, even having a signed contract doesn't always guarantee that all parties involved would fulfill their part of the arrangement.

But who gets to sign a contract with God? We usually don't feel the immediate consequence of not making good on our promises to Him. There's no judge to enforce our handshake agreement with God. And I won't even begin to pretend I know how God acts in every situation, but my experience has proved Him to be a pretty patient participant in these contracts we make with Him. As often as we violate the terms of these contracts, we usually don't experience the consequences of not meeting our side of the bargain as quickly as we would if we had a clear contract or written obligation signed by human participants. So, we conveniently forget to follow through on our side when we make promises to God, or even non-binding agreements with other humans.

But why is it so difficult to keep our promises? What happens to the guilt we feel when we don't fulfill our vows to God or to others? What are those thoughts we entertain that eventually convince us that it's okay not to do our part? Or are we just scared that we could decrease in some way if we meet those obligations?

There's an image that comes to mind when I think about Hannah's story, and keeping promises in general. This image depicts Jesus kneeling before a little girl with a big teddy bear behind His back as he requests for the little teddy bear in her hands. One can easily tell the girl in this picture is hesitant to give up her little teddy bear. But what she doesn't understand is that Jesus wants to trade her little bear for the bigger one behind His back. In this chapter, the little girl was Hannah. But you and I are this little girl as well. For Hannah, God wanted to trade her one thing for something bigger, but without courage, Hannah would have missed out on her reward. God already made good on His part of the deal, but He also wanted to do more for her.

There's something powerful and rewarding when we don't hesitate to keep our promises to people and God. We should want to keep our side of the bargain. Our first or final thoughts should never rest in a place where we're contemplating to default. When we decide to push past the fear-based thoughts that tell us to renege on our promises, the results are not limited to the avoidance of consequences. We suddenly find ourselves increased, in one form or another. With other humans, we suddenly find ourselves increased to higher levels of trust and integrity that enables greater interactions with our family, friends, employers, loan officers, landlord, etc. With God, we set ourselves up for bigger and better blessings. Obedience is better than sacrifice with Him.

We also should understand that making good on our end of the bargain blesses the receiver. The receiver is eager to receive their share of the agreement, and we deny them that joy, and even arouse anger, when we decide to withhold our vows. Samuel was born and made available for the Lord's use at the right time. Eli, the aging priest at the temple, had sons that were supposed to take over the priestly duties of their father. Unfortunately, they were unruly and undeserving of the role. But without a priest, who would communicate with God on behalf of the children of Israel? But with Samuel available, learning the ways of the elderly priest, and being responsive and obedient to the voice of God, he became a great prophet for the nation of Israel.

CHARACTER PROFILE
* Trustworthy
* Focused
* Faithful
* Consistent
* Honest

CHECK IT OUT!
1 Samuel Chapters 1 and 2

THE REWARD
* You can be rest assured that God will keep His end of the bargain. Not only did Hannah have the prayed-for son, she was blessed with five more.
* I'm sure her faith was increased when God answered her prayers for the Samuel. It wasn't hard for her to believe Him (God) for the other children.
* Her joy was full and all her years of being tormented by Peninnah became insignificant

- The children of Israel gained a great Prophet and Judge because one person courageously chose to keep her promise.

PONDER A BIT

- Why do you think we find it so easy to make promises but so hard to fulfill them?
- Have you ever reneged on a promise? What were some of the consequences to not keeping your promise?
- Who are the people most affected by unfulfilled promises?
- Why do we take the forgiving nature of God or others for granted
- How does one get better with fulfilling their promises
- What would you consider your most prized possession? What would it take to give up that one thing? What if God wanted you to give it up?

ACT NOW

1. Make a list of promises you've made to date. Cross out the ones you've fulfilled and indicate the dates (if you can) you took care of these items. For the ones yet to be crossed off, indicate when you plan on making good on these promises. Share with a trusted friend or loved one to help with accountability. Make a copy of the list, if needed. Tell them to check in with you a week or so before you need to fulfill the promise, just so you're reminded and/or are making progress towards the goal.
2. If you know a couple struggling with infertility, take some time to say a prayer for them. You can share that you're praying along with them, but you don't have to. I personally find joy in praying for others when they don't know I'm praying for them just because it takes me out of the picture while ascribing the glory to God.

EVEN MORE

Shade Sabitu

Chapter 5

Mordecai

Courage is being a valuable influence on someone

PICTURE THIS!

Susan had been working at the local credit union for the past three years and was recently offered a promotion as an operations manager. If you could only hear the thoughts in her head, you would understand why she was over the moon about this promotion. She worked so hard over the years and it felt good that her supervisor finally believed that she was up to the task of leading others. All she had to do now, she thought, was prove to everyone (but mostly herself) that she was able to handle the added responsibility.

For her, the challenge began as she tried to understand the needs of her new team. She understood her direct reports had differing levels of experience, as well as unique professional and personal goals. One individual, Carrie, saw her current position as perfectly suited for her lifestyle and was very content with how things were going in her career. She was juggling full-time work with part-time school and didn't have the time or desire to take on additional responsibilities at work. She was good at what she did and didn't mind continuing it for the next few years. Dan, on the other hand, was just a clock-puncher, showing up every day until he could earn enough money to pay for pilot school. That's what he really wanted to do.

But then there was the recent college grad, Jola, who wasn't quite sure where he wanted to go in his career. Susan knows how intelligent he is and that he has a genuine interest in learning more about the financial sector. But she also notices the lack of certain skills necessary for his progression at the credit union. Unfortunately, Jola doesn't know what he doesn't know, and without someone guiding him, he'll never make the progress required to climb that ladder. He's not saying any words, but his actions are practically screaming, "help me, teach me, mentor me, and guide me." Susan hears it, but what was she supposed to do about it?

She starts to think, "I could take Jola under my wing and mentor him. But what about my career? I mean, that's a major commitment! Not only will it require time; it will require patience, training, sponsorship, personal setbacks, reinforcement, feedback, and other emotional and physical resources that I could honestly expend on advancing my own career. Besides, I didn't have anyone to help me. I figured it out on my own. Jola should do the same. And what if it's all a waste? What if he doesn't appreciate my efforts? What if I expend all my resources and he fails anyway? What if he leaves within the next six months? That's my name and reputation on the line! It's a major risk I'm not sure I should take." Deep down though, Susan can't shake the feeling that she needs to help Jola because she knows he can't do this on his own.

Some folks come from disadvantaged backgrounds, with no clear guidance or example of success. There's no one to help them achieve their goals and dreams. Sometimes, these individuals know where they want to go but don't know how to get there.

Other times, they are simply unable to recognize the potential that others can so clearly see in them. Either way, they need someone, a mentor, to help guide them to success. Behind their seemingly confident smile is an insecurity that needs an outside voice to dispel.

This was the story of Mordecai. He took on the role of father to his baby cousin when she was orphaned. He was there to be her guide and a source of wisdom whenever she needed leadership. You too can be that for someone else. Who knows? Maybe you're where you are for such a time as this

———— ⚭   ⚭ ————

THE STORY

When Esther became an orphan, Mordecai, her cousin, took her in and raised her as his own daughter. It was never recorded that Mordecai had a wife or kids of his own, so we can safely assume he was living 'the bachelor life' before he had to take on the responsibility of caring for someone else. I can only imagine this change being a huge adjustment for him. But like Susan, he knew if he didn't step up and help Esther, she would be lost on her own and unable to realize her full potential. So, as a child is to a father, Mordecai made Esther his number one priority.

When Mordecai learned King Xerxes was looking for a new Queen, he just knew Esther would be perfect for the position. She had the beauty, composure, and personality to earn her that position. So, Mordecai entered her into the competition, and off Esther went to live in the women's quarters of the King's palace. But before she left, he instructed her not to reveal her heritage because he didn't want her, or anyone else, to view it as a limitation. She did exactly as advised. This ends up being some solid advice as we'll see later on. Interestingly, Mordecai didn't simply give his cousin some advice and let her go. Since he worked at the gate of the King's palace himself, he would pace in front of the women's quarters to ask after Esther's welfare - every day. Such a dad move.

As God would have it, Esther was the chosen one - the new Queen! All the people she met throughout the competition, and obviously the King himself, fell in love with Esther. It was a true rags to riches, grass to grace, Cinderella story. Except there was a lot of drama before the happy ending.

See, there was this guy named Haman who was promoted to Chief Advisor

45

to King Xerxes. With the promotion came mandated honor and respect from the other advisors and nobles in the King's courts. It was actually a decree from the King that all should honor Haman by bowing to him whenever he passed by them. But Mordecai refused to bow himself before Haman. The Bible doesn't explicitly say why Mordecai refused to bow before Haman, but some scholars believe Mordecai thought bowing before Haman would be contrary to Jewish customs or principles.

This blatant disobedience angered Haman so much that he wanted not only to punish Mordecai, but to kill every Jew alive. Talk about an ego trip. So, Haman started to devise a very wicked plan. He would manipulate the King and make him believe the Jews were a dangerous group of people that needed to be eliminated from the land. And by elimination, Haman meant the execution of every Jew. So, with his influence on the King, the decree was issued, and an execution date was determined.

Mordecai heard of the decree and suggested to Esther that she use her influence as Queen to cancel the decree. Remember when I mention that Esther was supposed to keep her heritage a secret? Well, as you've probably figured out by now, she was a Jew too! So, the decree would have her killed as well, if she didn't act fast.

At first, Esther was too scared to approach the King. She knew the proper palace etiquette was to wait for an invitation from the King before approaching his presence. Even as Queen, she couldn't just approach him whenever she felt like it. She was very aware that disobedience to this rule could lead to her death.

Well, with this new decree, she was going to die either way - whether she didn't intervene and just let the predetermined execution day happen, or if she approached the King without his invitation. At least, that's what Mordecai thought and tried to make his baby cousin understand. She had to summon the courage to approach the King. Too many lives were at stake. His encouragement helped her realize her power, influence, and ability to help her people at such a critical time. He gained her attention and made her realize the importance of her position and the potential result of her doing nothing.

I'm sure you can guess what happened next. She summoned the courage to approach the King, was warmly welcomed to speak with him, and made her request of the King. When Haman's plot was exposed, he was killed, and the Jews were saved. There's a lot more to this very interesting story and so much more to learn, so I encourage you to read the Book of Esther for more details.

COURAGE ON DISPLAY

The recurring challenge in this story was the need to resist being self-focused. There were a number of times Mordecai had to put others ahead of himself. He knew he could no longer care for himself and had to stand up to raise his baby cousin. He knew he had to risk being ostracized by his colleagues when he foiled an assassination plot against the King (not discussed here). He knew he couldn't just run away when he heard the decree; he had to protect the interests of his people. Overall, he constantly had to resist the urge to protect his own self-interests. With courage, he was able to use his influence to save the lives of many. And his courage and selfless thinking encouraged Esther to think likewise.

That was the beauty in what he did. He allowed his selflessness to breed courage in someone else. With Esther now empowered with the knowledge of the strength she possessed, she was able to break protocol and request safety for her people. Had Mordecai been only concerned about his own needs, the story would have taken a different turn.

What's that saying again? "With great power comes great responsibility". Mordecai, in this story, had great power. It may not seem like it, but his influence on Esther helped her fulfill her destiny. She was in a position of authority, but it was Mordecai's wisdom and guidance that encouraged her to face her fears. At times, we take for granted our ability to influence others. Children, spouses, colleagues, mentees, mentors, community leaders - these are all the people we can influence and inspire to go above and beyond. Not sharing your insights, words of encouragement, wisdom, and experience may delay someone else's growth. You don't need to be in a position of high prestige before you selflessly give of yourselves to others. Mordecai started off as just a cousin - but then he became a dad, advisor, and supporter for Esther.

Don't we sometimes forget how our own positions can help or hurt others? And isn't it great when someone comes along to remind us of our potential and influence? We need to remember that any of us can be the individual that challenges or prompts someone else to greatness. It takes wisdom, grace, humility, and much courage to check our own cares at the door and pursue the greater good for someone else. Isn't that the meaning of love? Love is courageous. Courage is powerful and being able to help others along their growth path can bring a personal fulfillment that material rewards can't buy.

CHARACTER PROFILE
- Selfless
- Passionate
- Wise
- Honest
- Thoughtful

CHECK IT OUT!

The Book of Esther

THE REWARD
- With Mordecai's help, Esther became Queen in a mighty kingdom.
- The life of the king was spared because Esther was Queen, had the ear of the king, and was able to speak for Mordecai and his efforts in foiling a deadly trap against the king. (I didn't talk about this in this chapter, but you can find it in the reference).
- Several lives were saved because of the bravery of one person (Esther) who was initially encouraged by another (Mordecai).
- Mordecai was in turn publicly honored for his loyalty and service to the king.
- Haman and all enemies of the Jews were destroyed.

PONDER A BIT
- What are the first thoughts that come to mind when you see someone in need, and you have the ability to help?
- What are the typical sacrifices that come with mentoring or helping others?
- What makes us see ourselves as unable to help others?
- Why do you think people equate someone else's success with their own failure?

ACT NOW

1. Think of one person you care about. It could be a friend, sibling, parent, child, colleague, or neighbor. Most likely, you know about their passions and personal goals. Ponder how you can contribute positively and wisely to them achieving one of those goals. It could be as simple as asking them about their progress on achieving that goal. Some people just need someone to keep them accountable. Another way to help could be stepping in to help with a particular chore so they can use that time to work on that project and get even closer to accomplishing something great. Whatever it is, the plan must be agreed upon with the recipient so they can also understand your intentions and its significance. You never know... your willingness to positively add to their lives may trigger them to want to do the same for someone

else. Remember, courage begets courage.

Even more

Chapter 6

Josiah

Courage is charting a new path

PICTURE THIS!

This year's family reunion was about to get very awkward. After two years in college, Casey noticed her worldview was changing a lot, and she wasn't sure if her family's belief system had kept up. She didn't know what to expect when we went off to school in a diverse city like Toronto. But she was delighted to have met so many people from such diverse cultural and religious backgrounds. The experience was forcing her to quit some preconceived notions of others.

But to make things more complicated, she had fallen in love with David, her tutor for Advanced Writing. You see, David was a Black guy from Nigeria and was the exact opposite of what her family members had said about Africans. For one, David was the most ethical guy she'd ever met. With him, everything was just so black and white – there was no gray. It was such a wide contrast to the story her father told about his friend that was duped by a Nigerian some 10 years ago. Her Uncle Phil also told of how he was sold counterfeit goods by a Ghanaian business partner. In their family, Africans were off limits because they couldn't be trusted.

These, however, weren't the only prejudice comments she'd heard over her developmental years. Her previous impression of different cultural and religious groups was far different from what she was experiencing in school. The fact that people were supposed to be in these small boxes created by her family was the kind of thinking she no longer wanted to entertain. She wanted her family to know where she stood on this issue and was willing to deal with any consequences, if necessary. She knew her own children would not have any of these limiting notions. And whether her family welcomed David or not was irrelevant. If they wanted to keep defining whole ethnic groups based on their limited experience with people of similar backgrounds, that was their problem. All she promised herself was to start with a blank slate when dealing with any individual.

Like Casey, the idea of starting a new legacy was what set Josiah apart during his reign as King. His father and grandfather ruled a certain way, and he could see the destructive consequences of their decisions. He wanted to go down a different path. But it was going to take some courage to direct the Kingdom in a new way of thinking. Let's explore how he did it.

THE STORY

Josiah became king when he was only 8 years old. Seriously! This wasn't one of those 'an 8-year-old was given a fictitious key to the city' situations either. He had legitimate power and authority over the people of Israel. Of course, he had counselors and advisors helping him out. But at the end of the day, he was allowed to have the final word. Aside from the numerous advisors at his service, he had another advantage going for him.

You see, he came from a long line of kings. His father was a king, and so was his grandfather, great grandfather, and so on. With his pedigree, acting, speaking, and thinking like a leader was probably more innate than it would be for a child with a less prestigious lineage. But regardless of social status or hierarchy in the community, most people will agree that a strong male presence can have tremendous influence in the lives of children, especially a male child.

In Josiah's lineage of kings, he had those that knew God, and obeyed His commands, and he had those that had complete disregard for God. Unfortunately for him, the ones who didn't care much for God were his immediate ancestors. His father and grandfather not only disobeyed God's instructions, they went out of their way to worship other gods. They went further and converted the temple of God to a place that held several altars for the worship of those other gods. Talk about adding insult to injury. And because of the blatant actions of disobedience and disregard, God not only punished these kings, he punished the whole nation of Israel along with them.

So, at age 16, Josiah decided he wanted to know more about God. Who was this God that his father (Amon) and grandfather (Manasseh) disregarded and disobeyed? Wasn't He the same God that his forefather King David served? Through the priests and prophets of God, he started to understand who God was and the personal and societal implications of serving other gods.

By age 20, he made sure all the wooden, engraved, and/or molded images created for these other idols were completely destroyed. At age 26, he ordered that the temple of God be repaired. In the midst of the construction, the Book of the Law, given to the children of Israel, but abandoned for decades, was found. The book was read to him and he suddenly understood how different God's will for the people were from the lives they were living. He requested for an assembly of all the inhabitants of the land. Once they were all gathered, Josiah publicly promised to serve God. The people, in turn, were instructed to make the same covenant, which they did. From that day on, no one was allowed to serve any other gods for the remainder of Josiah's reign.

Josiah then proceeded to re-initiate the Passover, a festival and celebration of the day the children of Israel were freed from slavery and allowed to leave Egypt.

It was a time to bless God for this miraculous liberation. After generations of unfaithful kings, the tradition was long forgotten. But Josiah made sure the people honored God with the celebration again. Therefore, the Passover was celebrated and was recorded to be the most elaborate Passover under any King in Israel.

COURAGE ON DISPLAY

It's pretty interesting the way the Bible explores Josiah's journey from a young boy to a man that feared and honored God. His story starts off with some background information on his family's circumstances and the decisions and actions that were taken before his conception. Like the rest of us, there was absolutely nothing Josiah could do regarding this aspect of his life. But then it goes on to describe a time when he began to show interest in something different.

His growth journey started with gaining the knowledge and understanding of his history and why things were the way they were. He also wanted to know who God was. "Why was God important and why were his forefathers so conflicted about him?" Once he had the information in hand, Josiah was convinced of his next steps. He didn't sit with knowledge in his head; he proceeded to take the necessary actions that reflected the condition of his heart.

There was something destructive about the way his father and grandfather ruled and led their kingdoms, and he didn't want to repeat history. He recognized that he had the power to correct the path his family was on, and he decided to use that power. He wanted to start a new legacy, one that acknowledged God and did away with idol worship.

This was ultimately what Josiah was known for. This was the legacy that made him stand out from his forefathers. The Bible records, *"Never before had there been a king like Josiah, who turned to the Lord with all his heart and soul and strength, obeying all the laws of Moses. And there has never been a king like him since."* (2 Kings 23:25 NLT)

You may not be a king, or have any type of leadership role. However, you still get to make certain decisions for yourself. What you decide when these questions or situations arise says a lot about who you are and the state of your heart. At different points in our lives, we're given the opportunity to tell ourselves and others where we stand on certain issues. And sometimes, our family members are the ones hardest to convince that our thoughts are not theirs.

Once your belief system differs from the pack, you suddenly become a lone wolf.

But this is where courage steps in to provide the comfort and strength to keep moving in the direction you want your life to move in. This is where you get to determine your own legacy and what statement(s) you want to make with your life. You can determine alcoholism stops with you; abuse stops with you; corruption and fraud stops with you; academic failure stops with you; poverty stops with you.

Yes, we may have a genetic disposition to certain behaviors, but that doesn't mean we lack the ability to overcome what may currently seem impossible to overcome. We always have a choice whether to sit back and let these behaviors happen to us or if we're going to courageously conquer the fear of "that's just who I am." It may, however, require another kind of courage to overcome ingrained thinking and behaviors. You may need the courage to humbly ask someone else to help you. Someone that will help you identify the better way of thinking and the resulting actions.

My advice? Start by asking God to lead you to the right people who will provide you with the best counsel. Once you know who that person (or people) is, be willing to change and ultimately win the battle of standing out and uniquely setting a new standard for yourself, your family, and generations to come.

CHARACTER PROFILE

- Curious
- Determined
- Unwavering

CHECK IT OUT!

2 Kings 21-23, 2 Chronicles 34-35

THE REWARD

- When Josiah was compared to the kings that were before him, and even those that came after him, he was known to serve God with all his heart. He knew what he believed, and he lived a life that exemplified his belief system. He made a name for himself and created a legacy that made his name great.

PONDER A BIT

- If you had to change one detrimental family tradition or custom, what would it be?
- What's the biggest challenge associated with breaking away from the pack and doing something different from other family members?
- Have you ever said to yourself, "I would never do/say *blank* to my own kids?" What were those words/behaviors? What about those words/behaviors do you dislike?
- What legacy do you want to leave behind for the next generation?

Act Now

1. Create two columns in your notebook. In the first, write out the things you love about your family's traditions and culture. Thank God for these ones. Also, thank your parents for showing leadership in these behaviors or ways of thinking. In the second column, write out the ones you dislike about your families' ideologies. On a new page, write down what you would change about these things. Think about the behaviors you can take to get you where you want to be. Think about the people that could mentor you to get there. Think about the company you need to keep to help you become who you want to be. Write all these things down and start with one thing and gradually incorporate the others. Record your successes and obstacles. What are you learning about yourself through this process? Who are those that are helping or could help? Focus on what you're doing right and the progress you're making to get to where you want to go.

Even more

Chapter 7

Ruth

Courage is loving selflessly and thoroughly

PICTURE THIS!

One day, my kids and I went over to the local library and borrowed some books to keep them occupied for a few weeks. They were starting to drive me crazy with the, "Mom, I'm bored" chant. One of the books I picked out for my youngest was called, *Babies Don't Walk, They Ride*, by Kathy Henderson. It's a great book for toddlers, with excellent illustrations and a lot to point at and talk about as you flip through the pages. As I read, I thought to myself, "Man, babies have it made!" Because, like the book points out, babies are able to get around the house, and around town, with little to no effort on their part. As an adult, there are days when that kind of life is something I envy.

But it wasn't just their sweet life that had me thinking. It was the fact that babies are effortlessly the recipient of selfless love and affection. They are showered with round the clock care and attention that is never dependent on what they can or can't do for their caregiver. Mothers and fathers have no expectation of these little ones. A simple toothless smile is usually reward enough. It's this kind of limitless selflessness that has caused people to make the baby-parent relationship the poster child of unconditional love.

But outside of this baby-parent relationship, is it possible for you and I to love someone else selflessly and unconditionally? Can we love knowing that love may not come back from that particular individual? Is it possible to put our own needs on the back burner and give ourselves to another without even the slightest expectation that the person, either now or later, will reward us for our loyalty? It may sound hard or even impossible to some, but this is the kind of love Ruth showed her mother-in-law, Naomi. Naomi had nothing to offer Ruth, yet Ruth remained loyal to their friendship. Let's learn more about Ruth and let her story inspire us to love selflessly.

THE STORY

The story of Ruth is a relatively short one, compared to our other characters. And unfortunately, it starts on a pretty grim note. Ruth, and another woman, Orpah, married two brothers who had lost their father a while back. After some time, both brothers also passed away, suddenly creating a situation where there were now three widows in one family – Ruth, Orpah, and their mother-in-law, Naomi. Back in those days, widows were a disadvantaged group. Without husbands or adult male children to fend for the family, widows often went without and were heavily reliant on the help and mercies of others.

Since Naomi was old and unable to care for herself or her daughters-in-law, she strongly encouraged them to go back to her birth towns. At least there, they could hopefully remarry and start new lives for themselves. Naomi (her husband and her sons) were from Bethlehem of Judah (Israelites), but Ruth and Orpah were Moabites. Orpah took the offer and returned back to be with her people. But despite the uncertainty of their future, Ruth was determined to stay with her mother-in-law. Who would take care of Naomi if both daughters-in-law returned back to their hometowns to start new lives? With Naomi advanced in age, it would be very difficult to survive as a widow. Ruth just couldn't let her mother-in-law spend the rest of her days with no help and no one to lean on.

So, Naomi and Ruth traveled to Bethlehem and devised a plan for survival. Ruth was going to scrape up whatever she could in the grain fields after the harvesters went through. You see, it was a commandment from God that the children of Israel would leave small portions of their fields unharvested so that the poor, foreigners, and widows amongst them could pick up leftover grain in these parts of the fields. It was God's way of making sure these disadvantaged groups were fed. With this knowledge in hand, Ruth and Naomi knew, at the very least, they would not starve.

But God was with Ruth. Her loyalty, devotion, and love for her mother-in-law was known to God and to those in the town. One of the days Ruth was scraping up the leftovers in the field, one of the field owners, Boaz, showed up and immediately took a liking to her. He not only ordered the harvesters to leave more grain behind when they went through the fields, he instructed Ruth to have lunch in his house and to eat and drink to her heart's content. She even took some lunch home to Naomi. Eventually, Boaz inquired to see if he could marry Ruth, and proceeded to make her his wife.

The rest, as they say, is history. Except in their story, the history they created was pretty significant. Boaz and Ruth went on to have a baby named Obed. Obed had a son called Jesse, and Jesse went on to birth King David himself! So, from one act of love and sacrifice came the birth of a generation of greatness. It's amazing what courage can birth in our lives, if and when we let it happen.

<hr/>

COURAGE ON DISPLAY

Like I said before, love is courageous. But it can also seem quite foolish at times. It seeks to give completely without considering what it can get in return.

I liken it to a farmer doing all the hard work of farming (planting, weeding, irrigating, fertilizing, etc.), but turning around and not caring if the fields yield any produce. Talk about a waste of energy, passion, resources, and time. But to love courageously is to be like this farmer. That is why Ruth's expression of love was so special...so courageous. Her seemingly foolish decision to put someone else's present needs ahead of hers displayed her willingness to abandon hoped for, but also unknown, future personal gains.

Staying with her mother-in-law was of no benefit to Ruth. The benefits of their new situation were going to be one-sided. Naomi had nothing to offer Ruth. And there was no guarantee of any future change to that situation. This was Ruth putting her life on hold for Naomi. There was no guarantee of a new husband, having her own kids, or having a steady source of income. All Ruth did was love Naomi in that moment, not minding what the future would or wouldn't have in store for them. I love how the Amplified version of the Bible describes Love. It describes it as seeking the greatest good for someone else. In Ruth's case, she was so focused on Naomi and her overall well-being, she didn't spend a second to think about how her sacrifice would play out for her own future.

Ruth knew she couldn't leave Naomi to fend for herself. When the widow was begging her daughters-in-law to move on with their lives, all Ruth could focus on was Naomi's own needs in that moment. Naomi knew Ruth and Orpah were young enough to start new lives, and didn't want them feeling pressured to hold themselves back for her. But knowing Naomi's predicament caused Ruth to pause in her steps. Her pause and willingness to stay with her mother-in-law showed her disobedience to fear. Fear was telling her to think about her own future. But courage told her that loving completely and selflessly was the 'higher' action to take.

From what I can deduce from the text, Naomi must have been pretty kind to her daughters-in-law. All three women wept at the thought of needing to part ways. And it's definitely easy to love someone that loves you back. But even when we love someone who loves us, is our love ever without condition or expectation? There's usually an expectation to receive something in return for our expressed love. And disappointment occurs when those expectations are not met.

But love doesn't focus on the reward. It only thinks of the present need. Wouldn't you know, though, that a reward always seeks out those situations where love is being completely and selfishly expressed. It's a given. Maybe that was the guarantee Ruth relied on. That's the guarantee we can all rely on. There's no need to call attention to yourself or tell the world you're loving someone selflessly. Nor do you need to wonder if all your efforts are for naught. God has a way of making sure your selfless love is crowned with glory. Our job is to not worry about the consequences of loving someone. They may abuse it, take it for granted, not acknowledge it, or even throw it away. But when we love completely, like Ruth did, we don't worry about the outcome; we focus on how our love helps the receiver. And we let the Great Rewarder take care of the rest.

<hr/>

CHARACTER PROFILE

- Loyal
- Selfless
- Stubborn
- Confident
- Hardworking
- Fearless
- Strategic
- Enterprising

CHECK IT OUT!

The Book of Ruth Chapters 1 through 4

THE REWARD

- Naomi and Ruth moved past the typical mother-in-law/daughter-in-law relationship to become great friends.
- The story of Ruth's goodness to her mother-in-law was heard throughout the land, and this brought her favor with Boaz. Once Boaz knew she was surviving on other people's leftovers, he made sure Ruth had much more than she needed. Therefore, as widows, Ruth and Naomi never went without.
- Ruth remarried and had a baby with Boaz. This baby became the grandfather of King David, great grandfather of King Solomon, and forefather of King Josiah. Therefore, a lineage of greatness was born out of Ruth's complete loyalty to Naomi.

PONDER A BIT

- What does sacrificial love look like to you?
- What is one way you've loved sacrificially?
- Most of us are loved when we love. But have you ever loved someone so dearly but was rewarded with harshness?

- Because Naomi had nothing to offer Ruth, Ruth didn't have an expectation of being rewarded for her loyalty to Naomi. Why do people have an expectation to be rewarded for their good acts?
- What are some ways we can focus on the act of giving without an expectation for a reward?
- How can we express love to someone that may not appreciate our sacrifice of love?

Act Now

1. Loving selflessly is not as hard as it sounds. It can be as simple as doing something good for someone without expecting a reward in return. But it also means doing something that will 'cost' you something. It doesn't need to be money. It just needs to be something that will mean a lot to you and to the recipient. Make a list of such things. It doesn't need to be done now, but you should revisit this list often and cross out the ones you've been able to achieve as they happen.
2. If you've been good to another in the past, and that good was unappreciated, pray to God and ask Him to help you think of those good deeds as sacrificial love. That way, you can let go of the hurt and expectations associated with those actions.
3. Remember, Love never expects anything in return, but it is never unrewarded.

Even more

Chapter 8

Jonah

Courage is righting wrongs

PICTURE THIS!

Terry hated herself now. She hated what she had become. She hated that she felt helpless and unable to change where her life was headed. They had their problems, but nothing particularly unique to them. She still loved her husband dearly. But no matter how hard she wanted to, she found herself unable to resist Mark, a guy she works with and has been having an affair with for the last two years. Her husband, Rich, is unaware of her infidelity, and if he were to ever find out, that would be the end of their marriage. She didn't want to end up divorced like her parents and her sister. But from where she was sitting, it couldn't end up any other way.

"Why can't I just stop seeing Mark," she wonders. She knew her marriage could be salvaged, if she ended the affair. And she knew her relationship with Mark was just a matter of opportunity. They both traveled together for work, and things just happened. Her husband, on the other hand, was a dream come true for her. All her friends were jealous that she married such a caring guy. Though Rich wanted kids, she didn't. But he never pressured her on the topic. Maybe that's why she convinced herself she could never truly be enough for him. Maybe that's why she was self-sabotaging her relationship.

In her mind, time was running out and there was nothing left to do but watch everything crumble. The harm was done, the sin committed, and she waited too long to stop things from falling apart. But as we'll learn, through the story of Jonah, we can always turn things around. We don't need to keep moving in a direction that leads nowhere. We don't need to surrender to hopelessness. We get to choose life - every day. We can always correct our path and right our wrongs.

THE STORY

The Christian faith is heavily reliant on the need to believe. We need to believe God is God, that He created all things for His good pleasure, that He does as He pleases with His creation, that He loves us, and that He's able to do the most impossible things through and for us. Without these basic beliefs, it's hard to fully appreciate what we read and come across in the Bible. The Bible is full of stories of the incredible acts of God, some easier to grasp than others.

One of the many improbable stories is that of Jonah and the Big Fish. Even if you're not a Christian, you've probably heard some form of this story. Some guy being swallowed up by some sort of big fish or whale and being spit up after three whole days.

To be honest, believing such a story, even for a person of faith, requires a whole bunch of faith. But if you can believe the Boston Red Sox could come back to win the World Series after an 86-year old curse, I challenge you to believe God can use even a fish to bring salvation to His children. Yeah, I know it's a stretch, but stay with me here. I challenge you to open your heart to this seemingly improbable story - one in which a man's life is saved by a big sea creature.

But before we jump into the story, I want to ask you one question. How hard is it for you to give someone bad news? Nobody wants to be the boss that has to lay someone off, or the police officer that tells a wife that her beloved husband died in a fatal car accident. Nobody wants to be the bearer of bad news. Well, prophets and/or messengers of God frequently were that guy. Just because the message came from God didn't make it any easier to deliver.

Jonah, a messenger of God, was asked to deliver a pretty grime message to a large city of people whose lives displeased God. Imagine if the whole city of New York was told they were going to be destroyed in 40 days because of all the things they've done. The Bible doesn't detail exactly what they did, but for God to want to destroy a whole city, I'm not sure any of these folks would be considered nice or friendly. Would you want to be the guy to deliver that message? Probably not.

So, like you and I, Jonah decided, "uh yeah...I'm going with a 'no' on this one, God." So, he bought a boat ticket and headed in the opposite direction, to a place called Tarshish. It was like booking a ticket to San Francisco instead of heading to New York. He thought he was running from God. But God was not having any of this disobedience. So, He made Jonah's boat trip very uncomfortable. And by uncomfortable, I mean God caused the seas to be especially tumultuous that day, enough for all those on the ship to fear for their lives and begin to call out to their respective gods to rescue them.

All except Jonah, that is, who was in a deep sleep within the boat and completely unaware of the turmoil that was going on outside. The other sailors woke him up and requested that he pray to his own god too, in hopes that his god would be the divine being to save them from their impending deaths.

The sailors then decided to draw straws in an attempt to find out whose sin was the cause of the terrible storm. And wouldn't you know, Jonah drew the short straw. They asked Jonah to identify himself and ask what he could have done to bring such calamity upon himself and the rest of them on the boat. He responded by telling them who his God is and how he had disobeyed God's instructions. They then asked him what they should do with him to appease his god. His response? "Throw me overboard and the storm will cease." They hesitated. How could they throw a man overboard in the middle of the sea? However, after Jonah's continued insistence and after the men said a prayer of forgiveness for the sin they were about to commit, the sailors threw Jonah overboard. As soon as he hit the waters, the storm seized. In complete awe, the sailors believed in Jonah's God, worshipped Him, and swore their lives to Him. Not the point of this chapter, but it goes to show you that God can even use our disobedience to glorify Himself. The order of events could only be orchestrated by the one true God.

As for Jonah, God caused a big fish to swallow him up. The swallowing wasn't to kill him though. The belly of the fish was just a place to hold Jonah for three days and three nights. While in the fish, Jonah reached out to God in prayer. His prayer was that of thanksgiving because God had used the fish to save his life. After the three days, God caused the fish to spit Jonah up on a seashore. Once on shore, God spoke to Jonah, as He did before, and ordered him to go to Nineveh to warn the people of the pending doom. This time, he headed straight to Nineveh and delivered the message. The people heard the warning and quickly repented. God heard their prayers and forgave them of their sins. So, because Jonah redeemed himself and did the right thing, a whole city of people was saved.

<hr>

COURAGE ON DISPLAY

Most people have internal signals that go off once we know we've done something wrong. At times, we're quick to silence the alarm, like hitting the snooze button in the morning, temporarily ignoring the notification. But be rest assured, the alarm will come back with full vengeance! Like Jonah, we can't expect to run away from our wrongs forever. Those temporary escapes are just that - temporary. The wrong things we've done always seem to find their way back to us until we find the strength and courage to deal with them.

What I've realized, however, is how difficult it is to correct my path even when I know I've done something wrong. "When you know better, do better!" It's a saying I've heard several times and seems like such easy advice to take. But oh, how I wish it were that easy. Even when the consequences are slapping me across the face, I find myself putting my head down instead of turning my whole body around.

I've wondered what could be at the root of this struggle of not doing better when I've already figured out the better to do. Then I figured it out. The root of this constant struggle is fear. It may be disguised as so many other things (ignorance, pride, selfishness) but it is ultimately known as fear. And as we've learned by now, courage is the one thing that can displace fear.

Let's say, for example, you've falsely testified against someone, and the person is now sentenced to jail time. You could own up to the offense, and possibly alter this person's life trajectory. But then, suddenly, a number of fears show up: fear of being known as a liar, fear of retaliation, fear of the repercussions of perjury. So, because these fears rear their ugly heads, you stay quiet, but are constantly alarmed to the wrong done. It suddenly takes an act of courage to right this wrong.

But like Jonah, we're always given the time to reflect on our past wrongs, and for the most part, shown what those corrective steps should be. Jonah was stuck in the belly of the fish for three days and nights, plenty of time for him to regret his disobedience to God and decide that Nineveh was definitely better than where his sin led him. Smelly fish, Nineveh; Nineveh, smelly fish. Making the right choice and deciding the next step to take for Jonah was probably not as hard as the ones you and I debate in our heads. It's only courage, however, that will push you and I to take the corrective steps we know we must take.

Some believe they're lost causes, and therefore stay on the wrong path because they have no hope of doing better for themselves. But with all due respect, this belief system is cowardly. When I think of people who have the power, but choose not to change their situations, I envision a person rocking back and forth in a comfy old rocking chair, humming loudly to drown out the despair that starts to creep up on their inside. There's no amount of rocking or humming that will replace the need to get up and take some corrective actions.

Sometimes we may need a little push off that chair though. And there's something very courageous about humbling oneself and asking for help. Jonah knew he was wrong, and he probably felt like he deserved to die in the horrible storm. He didn't deserve to be shown mercy and to be spared his life. But that didn't stop him from approaching his Heavenly Father and asking Him to save his life. He knew God could turn his situation around, if only he was brave enough to ask. If we find ourselves wanting to change but unable to do it on our own, asking, receiving, and acting upon the help we need will get us to where we need to be.

"I would have despaired had I not believed that I would see the goodness of the LORD In the land of the living." (Psalms 27:13 AMP). This verse is one of my favorites because it helps me believe that things will get better. For someone

trying to turn their life around, it's a source of encouragement that the corrective efforts are worth the sweat and tears that will occur to make things right.

So yes, turning around and taking the right steps in the right direction will be hard. I can almost guarantee that. But the journey will be worth it. Staying in the current destructive path also has its own guarantee - destruction. But changing paths not only avoids the guaranteed destruction but gives hope for a much better outcome. So, let's take the steps together. Let's ask for help. Let's have courage for the consequences of the new path. And let's get ready for a new and better life.

CHARACTER PROFILE
- Stubborn
- Grateful
- Strong

CHECK IT OUT!
Jonah 1-3

THE REWARD
- A whole city was saved from destruction because Jonah had the courage to deliver the warning from God.

PONDER A BIT
- What are some other reasons why we don't just turn around when we know we're going down the wrong path?
- Who are the people in your life that can help you identify the corrective path for your mistake(s)?
- What would motivate you to change directions in your life?

ACT NOW
1. There are things we may have done wrong that require more courage to correct than others. List out the ones you believe you can easily correct. Find someone that can boost your confidence but will also hold you accountable to making the corrective actions. Put down timelines as to when you want the corrective path identified and when you want to make the said amendments. Share this with your identified accountability partner. Work through your list and update your partner

with the progress.

EVEN MORE

Epilogue

The beautiful thing about courage is that you can start expressing it today. No formal training required. The ability to achieve those courageous acts are already in you. So, my challenge to you is to seek it out. Take the time for self-reflection. This is something most of us don't take enough time to do. But because you're on this journey called courage, you need to make the time to learn about yourself. Understand what it is that makes you unique. Understand what courage will look like for you. Understand the things that have intimidated you in the past. Seek out the path that will get you where you want to be.

How do you find that path? Well, you need to ask for directions. You wouldn't go to a new place without seeking help in the form of a map or the use of a navigation system, would you? Therefore, you need to seek out the resources that will guide you on your way. Identify that leader or potential mentor with the insights on handling your current areas of intimidation or fear. They've probably been through similar situations before and were able to navigate it successfully. Or maybe they didn't succeed but were able to identify the pitfalls on the way and can therefore give you a roadmap that identifies those obstacles. With their guidance, you'll know where those obstacles are and can navigate around them, making your path easier and more successful.

Personally, the more I learn about myself, the more I find myself wanting to know more about God. After all, He was the one who made me, and therefore knows why and how He created me. He knows those unique traits in me to accomplish those things purposed for me to conquer. So, how could I ever dream of succeeding on this journey of courage without leaning into the One who created and possesses the roadmap of my life?

I therefore also encourage you to seek out the help of your Maker. No one else knows more about a product than the manufacturer. Knowing Him means knowing yourself and your purpose. In times of prayer and meditation, you'll be amazed at how God will reveal yourself to you. But it all starts with a personal declaration that you believe in Him and His power to do great works of courage in and through you. Confess that you no longer want to do things your way, and that His will for your life is what you desire.

If you're ready to make that your declaration, repeat the following: Lord, thank you for your love and grace, and your desire to do great works in and through me.

I confess my sins and no longer desire to live a life that is self-serving, but a life that is courageous and purpose-fulfilling. Lord, take control of my life and let my life please you. Reveal myself to me and lead me on the path I should go. Thank you because I know from now on, Your Holy Spirit will always be with me from this point forward. In Jesus name I pray. Amen.

If you made that declaration, I welcome you to a newer and greater phase in your life. Have an expectation to see your life transform in a more purposeful way. Be ready to take some bold steps and see old situations in a new light. Observe the changes in your thinking and take note of how it will change the outcome of your day-to-day activities. Share your thoughts with me or your spiritual mentor and let's continue to grow together on this new and exciting journey. Cheers to your coming success!

Acknowledgements

I thank the Sovereign God for the opportunity to share these words of wisdom with the world. I'm grateful for my life and the grace to express my own form of courage. I'm also grateful for the people God has put in my life to help me identify my courage.

I thank my loving husband, Temitope, and beautiful children, Ore, Rayo, Rola, for helping me recognize that I have the courage to love and sacrifice for others completely. My life is full with you all as my blessings. I love you all!

I thank my father, Henry Igbekele Owosela, for helping me recognize that I have the courage to write and communicate meaningful thoughts to the world. I couldn't have prayed for a better father. I love you Daddy!

I thank my mother, Elizabeth Anike Owosela, whom God assigned to birth me and raise me. A mother like no other, who stands by me and helped me to recognize early enough that I have the courage to serve others with love. You are an amazing example of how to love and serve others and I love for you that...and for many more reasons.

I thank my siblings (Tope, Kayode, Dami, and Jide) for always being my best friends. I will always love you all.

To all my dear friends and loved ones - you know yourselves - thank you for encouraging me to achieve greatness. We're going higher together guys!

To my editor and book designer, Amelia and TemitOpe, I couldn't have accomplished this without you guys. Thank you so much for your dedication and diligence.

And finally, I thank YOU for picking up this book. My prayer for you is that you start (or continue) to find ways to be courageous and inspire others to do the same in the name of my Lord, Jesus Christ.

References

1. https://allpoetry.com/poem/14519824-Promises-And-Dreams-by-C.-J.-Krieger

2. https://www.familyfriendpoems.com/poem/keeping-the-promises

www.ingramcontent.com/pod-product-compliance
Lightning Source LLC
Chambersburg PA
CBHW071632040426
42452CB00009B/1596